just walking

To
Pastor + Carol Schaad
Jeremiah 6:16
May God bless you
as you walk with Him.

Della Camp

just walking

LIVING
INK
BOOKS™
Writing Worth Reading™

clella camp

ISBN 0-89957-134-4

First printing—February 2005

Cover designed by Market Street Design, Inc., Chattanooga, Tennessee
Interior design and typesetting by Reider Publishing Services,
    West Hollywood, California
Edited and proofread by Amanda Sorenson of Sorenson Communications,
    Dan Penwell, Sharon Neal, and Rick Steele
Black & white photos by Ruth E. Used by permission

Printed in Canada
11 10 9 8 7 6 5 –T– 8 7 6 5 4 3 2 1

These writings are dedicated to the people who have walked with me in life:

My mother who taught me to walk physically and spiritually;

My husband who has walked by my side for the past fifty years, even when the road was rough;

My children who have brought me the greatest joy because they have both walked beyond me spiritually;

My in-law children who have become as my own and have walked as a true part of our physical and spiritual family;

My grandchildren, who are following me and will soon pass me by in their spiritual walk;

May God bless all of you as you have blessed me.

This is what the Lord says:
"Stand at the crossroads and look;
ask for the ancient paths,
ask where the good way is,
and walk in it."

—Jeremiah 6:16

CONTENTS

Acknowledgments

My gratitude and great respect to Dan Penwell, editor at AMG, who taught me, encouraged me, and believed in me.

My love and thanks to Teresa who kept saying, "You can do this, Mom."

And to Kaatje, my other daughter, who thought everything I wrote was good.

This book is a result of their faith in me.

My thanks also to:

Amanda Sorenson, copy editor—you made my writing readable. You taught this teacher!

Sharon Neal and Rick Steele for your professional proofreading expertise—you watched over my jots and tittles.

Kristy Speece, Gloria Mezera, and Connie Houston for critiquing and proofreading.

Suzette Stone for always encouraging and loving me.

The librarians at the Paris Carnegie Public Library for helping with research.

TO THE BRIDGE AND BACK

I TREAD A particular path to the bridge and back, no farther. I have been walking this route for several years now, so it really isn't too difficult. Some days I go a little faster, some a little slower. At times I'm a little stiff and the path seems harder. Other times I'm there and back in no time at all. If I haven't walked for a few days, I find it harder to get started, but whatever the reasons, I go only to the bridge and back. I don't push myself to go another step—just to the bridge and back. I know I am unduly proud that I have this routine in my life; but still, I sometimes boast to people when they are discussing the benefits of exercise that I walk to the bridge and back every day. I am rather quick to point out that many people my age don't do as much. It is my routine—to the bridge and back.

My Christian walk, at times, is much the same. I tread a particular path. Like my physical walk, I do the same things I have always done. I don't explore new paths, nor do I try to go any farther. Going beyond the "bridge" would mean I would have to push myself to learn something new, to talk to someone I haven't talked to before, to go into new territory.

When I do the things I have always done and stay in my little circle of comfort, I am quite content. I rationalize that God really doesn't expect any more of me—does he!? After all, I am doing more than many people do. My friends and family seem satisfied with what I am doing. I am a good Christian woman and maintain my Christian faith much like I maintain my physical body. I don't push myself to do any more than I have done for years. I'm not deteriorating, but unfortunately, neither am I increasing in my strength or my faith. Just to the bridge and back does the same thing for my faith as it does for my physical body.

PRAYER FOR TODAY

Lord, help me to cross the bridge of self-satisfaction. Push me to cross over whatever bridges you provide and to walk farther down the road of service. Help me to call, or care, or create just a little more than I did yesterday.

Ask where the good way is and walk in it,
and you will find rest for your souls.
—Jeremiah 6:16

ADDITIONAL SCRIPTURE READING

Deuteronomy 5:32, 33; Proverbs 4:12; Micah 6:8

TEN BENEFITS OF WALKING

- Burns calories
- Strengthens back muscles
- Easy on your joints
- Lowers blood pressure
- Shapes and tones legs
- Lowers cholesterol
- Reduces risk of heart disease and diabetes
- Relieves stress
- Improves attitude and mood
- Improves sleep

"All truly great thoughts are conceived by walking."

—FRIEDRICH NIETZSCHE (1844–1900), German philosopher and poet

⇒ 2 ⇐

FOG

I AM WALKING in the fog this morning. There is no sound. No birds are singing, no leaves are rustling, no dogs are barking in the distance. It isn't just quiet; it is nothing. The air is heavy. I struggle to breathe freely. Each step forward is a labored effort. Because I am on my daily path, I am having no problem with my footsteps, but the world around me is just not there.

The cornfield I walked by yesterday and the pipes for the new water line that were laid last week are not visible. I know they are there, but I can't see them. My conscious mind tells me all is the same as it was yesterday morning. I know that, but I don't feel it! Right now I feel only that I am alone in this world of nothingness. I struggle to get home one step at a time. If I stop, I think I could be lost even though I am on my everyday route and the way is so familiar.

Grief feels like this fog. So do loneliness and discouragement. As I reach the security of my driveway and turn toward the house, I think about the people around me who walk daily in a fog of emotions similar to what I am physically experiencing this morning. Most of them know that the world is out there going on around them, but they feel strangely out of touch. Day after day they put one foot in front of the other, walking their normal path because the routine of life must go on. Though they walk in a dense, emotional, and perhaps spiritual fog, they still walk. How difficult it is to feel lost and alone when you are walking a familiar path.

The Scripture teaches us to "bear one another's burdens," yet how often have I walked right by someone who was in the fog of loneliness or grief? How comforting it would have been this morning if someone had appeared beside me on that foggy road and walked with me for a while. How much more comforting it would be to have a companion walking beside us on that lonely path through the dense spiritual or emotional fog. Remembering our own foggy times can often help us come alongside a fellow traveler who is struggling through the foggy mornings of life.

PRAYER FOR TODAY

Lord, help me to recognize when a fellow walker is lost in the fog of grief, loneliness, or discouragement. Give me the insight and the ability to walk with others in the fog. Help them to press on until your Son can lift their particular fog, whatever it might be.

*Carry each other's burdens and in this
way you will fulfill the law of Christ.*
—Galatians 6:2

ADDITIONAL SCRIPTURE READING

Psalm 68:19; Matthew 11:28–30

"Angels whisper to a man when he goes for a walk."

—RAYMOND INMAN, author

ON THE TREADMILL

TODAY IS WHAT I call a treadmill day. It is another cold, rainy day with no sun in sight, but still I must walk. My treadmill is in our damp, dreary basement accompanied by the odor of drains, wet towels and leftover winter coats. Our basement is a holding place for the furnace, the water heater, and all the useless items we really should throw away, but can't just yet. When he was a small child, one of our grandsons called it *the dungeon.*

My treadmill runs only one speed because something is broken, and that speed is a little faster than I would like. Nevertheless, I need to walk so I step on and tread—one foot, then the other. My treadmill walk offers no scenery, no fresh air, no neighbors waving, no birds singing. My goal is three miles, and after a time I glance at the odometer anticipating it will read 2.75 miles by now. I have been going really fast, haven't I? It flashes a disappointing 1.6. I pull the handle and stop. There must be a better way than this to get my exercise! I head for the mall!

I have treadmill days in life too. Sometimes I have several in a row—one right after another. My walk is dreary; there is no light, and my environment "smells." I only have one speed—too fast. Just like my treadmill in the basement, something is broken, and I can't seem to slow it down. I can't get off without falling, so I just keep plodding, one foot in front of the other. I think I'm making progress because I'm going so fast, but when I check my progress, I find I'm not accomplishing my goals very quickly at all.

I am convinced there is a better way to live than just putting one foot in front of the other as fast as possible. So I pick up my Bible and read God's Word. I sing my favorite hymn—"Count Your Blessings." I watch my grandchildren play. I visit the nursing home, the hospital, or volunteer at church. I remind myself, "Be still and know that I am God." Going too fast isn't such a problem as long as I know that God is with me. I can walk on the treadmill (even if it is geared a little faster than I want) if I can remember why I'm walking. It also helps to change my scenery and walk in a different environment. Once I focus my attention out of myself and into God's way I have a smoother and easier walk even when the day is dreary and the environment around me is smelly.

PRAYER FOR TODAY

Lord, help me to walk in your way and to know that even in the dreary times of life you are with me to guide and support me.

Be still before the Lord.
—Psalm 37:7

ADDITIONAL SCRIPTURE READING
Psalm 46:10; 1 Thessalonians 4:11, 12

"Take a two mile walk every morning before breakfast."

—PRESIDENT HARRY TRUMAN (Advice on how to live to be 80)

≥ 4 ≤

JUST TO CHAT

THE BLINKING message light on my telephone answering machine greets me as I step through the doorway. I quickly push the button to hear what might be an urgent message I missed while walking. The stilted, computerized voice on the machine reports that I have two new messages. I anticipate the first and am not disappointed. It is the familiar and always welcome, "Hi Mom, it's just me" of my daughter's voice. She tells me that I haven't fixed my machine since the last time, but the main thrust of her message is that she really didn't want anything. She had just called to chat and would be gone all day but might call me back later.

I punch the button for message number two, and my daughter-in-law's voice drawls, "Hello." She informs me that she doesn't really want anything and had just called to chat and fill me in on the latest news in her life. She asks me to continue to pray for a mutual friend, tells me her plans for the day, where she can be reached, and says she will talk to me later.

As I leave the answering machine to begin my daily chores, I think how pleased I am as a mother that each of them called me *just to chat* and that neither of them really wanted anything. They just felt the need to touch base and chat before they started their busy day. They also know how much I appreciate their keeping in touch even though we don't live that far from one another.

I wonder if God might have the same type of response when I go to him to chat, to touch base and keep him informed about my plans for the day. So many times when I call on him, I have a need or a want, but I very seldom go to him and say, "Hi God, it's me. I really don't want anything. I just came to talk with you." As parents, we are so pleased when our children keep in touch with us on a regular basis. I can't help but think how much more pleased our heavenly Father must be when we have the same kind of relationship with him. I know how much I miss talking with my children when we don't have any contact for a few days. Short conversations when they need something really don't replace a long chat about the everyday things of their lives. God must miss me when I don't take the time to chat with him too.

PRAYER FOR TODAY

Help me Lord, to remember just to talk with you even when I don't want something. Thank you, Lord, for always being there to listen. Thank you for giving me children who keep in touch with me. Help me to be that kind of child for you.

Pray continually.
—1 Thessalonians 5:17

ADDITIONAL SCRIPTURE READING
Proverbs 15:8; Ephesians 6:18; Colossians 4:2

STRETCHING POINTERS

Warm up for a short time before stretching. Never stretch cold muscles because doing so may cause a torn muscle. A stretch should feel good, not painful. Slowly stretch to the point where you feel tension in the muscle. Quick jerks are not stretching and may result in injury.

"We make the path by walking."
—ROBERT BLY, Preface, *Iron John*

NO TRESPASSING

NO TRESPASSING signs are posted at intervals along the woods near my home. I see them every morning. I know it is illegal to walk in those woods, yet I have been there before. I know I should stay on the road and walk my usual path, but I also know how much I enjoy walking in the forbidden woods. I can walk by them for several days, but because I am weak and human, I eventually find myself turning into the driveway that leads me to the forbidden path.

Some people would not be tempted to trespass here at all. The dirt paths, the small animals, the dusky light, and the quiet surrounding would mean nothing to them. The NO TRESPASSING sign would offer little, if any, temptation. But for me it is different. Each time I walk there, I promise myself that I won't do it again. I recognize that I am breaking the law. I have been in the woods before, and I have seen the scenery. There isn't any reason for me to go back again and again, but I do.

My yearning for the forbidden woods reminds me of what the apostle Paul and I have in common: "I do not understand what I do. For what I want to do I do not do, but what I hate I do" (Rom. 7:15). Isn't that the truth? Many of us have been to places in life that we don't need to return to, yet we find ourselves drawn to that very thing— whether it is an undesirable habit, a friend, or a pastime.

As I walk on the forbidden path through the woods, I think of all the times in my Christian life that I have gone back to forbidden places I have been. The paths are different for each of us. For me, the path of worry is always tempting. Impatience and frustration with other people can often cause me to go down the path of anger even when I really don't want to. One of the paths I have worn smooth is the path of self-satisfaction. The habit of thinking—*I'm a lot better than a lot of other people because at least I'm walking.* Many of my fellow Christians walk this well-worn path with me.

I can ignore these forbidden paths quite well for several days, but eventually I find myself in the woods again. Just when I think I'm lost or that the owner will discover I am walking in his woods, I see an inviting patch of sunlight and rediscover the blacktop road I had left earlier. When I step out of the woods and onto the road, I know I have done it again. I have sinned against the owner of the property.

The amazing fact is the owner will forgive me for trespassing. When I confess to him (the next time I meet him) that I have left the road and ignored his NO TRESPASSING signs he will be kind and forgiving. The same is true of our heavenly Father. When I am treading the path of sin in the woods of the world, I become aware of my mistake. I see the light of Jesus and turn back to the road I was walking down previously. I know my Father forgives me. I am strengthened to continue my walk for another day.

PRAYER FOR TODAY

Father, keep me from turning onto the paths I have walked before that I know are not mine to walk on. Help me to walk the path of righteousness and to be an example for those who are following in the paths I tread each day.

For what I want to do I do not do, but what I hate I do.
—Romans 7:15

ADDITIONAL SCRIPTURE READING

Psalms 38:18; Proverbs 3:5, 6; 1 John 1:9

"To err from the right path is common to mankind."

—SOPHOCLES (AD 406–496?) Greek dramatist

⇒ 6 ⇐

WALKING IN THE DARK

I WOKE THIS morning to the predawn chirping of the birds roosting in the tree by my bedroom window. I lay there for a while and then decided to get dressed and walk, as my sleep for the night was obviously finished. I walk my familiar, everyday route, but walking in the dark that comes before morning generates an entirely different environment. I feel just a smidgeon of fear. Why would that be? I suppose it is the darkness. Darkness always creates strangeness, even in well-known territory.

I have never liked the dark. Objects look bigger in the dark, and the sounds of the night take on a heightened volume that is unheard in broad daylight. I think of the times I have lain in the dark of my bedroom and heard the scratching of what I believed was surely a huge rat, only to discover after some *brave* searching by my suddenly awakened husband, that a leaf was brushing the window. I have that same feeling now as I hear something in the weeds of the ditch next to the road. Why did I decide to do this?

I didn't give much thought to how dark it really was when I started, and I thought it would be no problem because I am in familiar territory. But as I continue, the sound of the wind in the trees begins to intensify and swirls of dirt from the plowed fields loom like black clouds in the road ahead of me. My smidgeon of fear is no longer lurking in the corners of my mind; it has grown into full-blown fright! I turn back, even though I have not reached the bridge (my daily turning point), increase my hesitant pace to a quick jog, and arrive breathless in my driveway. Home . . . safe!

My misadventure reminds me of how I often walk in the dark spiritually. Many mornings I start my day without prayer. I have no especially important plans for the day—just the ordinary household chores and errands, and in my impatience I don't take the time to talk with the Lord. I fully intend to have some quality time with him a little later in the day. So I plod through my morning routine with a halfhearted, apathetic attitude, and then wonder why my life is so dreary. I'm walking familiar territory, but there is no sparkle, no light in my day.

Just as the darkness created a different environment for my morning walk, so does the lack of prayer make a different environment for my day's activities. Without the light of prayer, I become tense and frustrated. Every little hindrance becomes a major issue. Dark clouds of despair and worry cluster in my mind. Much like my fear of the darkness, everything becomes bigger and more important than it should be. I run for safety. I stop, I pray.

I don't know why I postpone prayer. Past experience clearly shows that praying before I start my day renders an easier, happier day for me and all those around me. A day without prayer is much like walking down a familiar road in the dark: every little thing, even the ordinary things, becomes bigger and more intimidating.

PRAYER FOR TODAY

Forgive me, Lord, for days I start without coming to you. Forgive me for thinking that I am capable of handling my day without asking for your guidance. Thank you for all the times you have watched and helped even though I thought it was too unimportant or I was too busy to pray.

You, O Lord, keep my lamp burning;
my God turns my darkness into light.
—Psalm 18:28

ADDITIONAL SCRIPTURE READING

Psalm 32:7; Jeremiah 29:12; Colossians 4:2

WALKING MISTAKES

- Overstriding
- Wrong shoes
- Flapping or slapping feet
- Not using arms
- Swinging arms across the body
- Head down
- Leaning (forward, back, swaying)
- Wrong clothes
- Not drinking enough
- Overtraining (even God rested)

—Wendy Baumgardner (*Guide to Walking*, www.walking.about.com)

⋙ 7 ⋘

THE DEER STORY

JUST AS I STEPPED around the curve in the road, there they stood—two deer. As I move into view, their heads jerk up; their ears perk; their eyes focus; their nostrils flare; and then off they go. For just a few moments, I see their white tails bouncing as they jump over each row of soybeans growing along the wooded area that is home to them at night. I walk more slowly and think of last week's meeting at the church. Our deer hunter son spoke about change. Several times this week I have pondered his words, and seeing the deer reminded me again of the illustration that had made such an impression on me.

Our son had told the story of a veteran deer hunter who decided to take the time to teach his young child to hunt. Incident after incident revealed the older leader's direction and the young child's mistakes. At times the need was for following, and the child ran on ahead. At times the need was for quiet, and the child was noisy. At times the need was for slowness, and the child was quick. At times the need was for alertness, and the child was groggy. At times the need was for patience, and the child was impatient. Even so, the veteran hunter continued struggling, walking, teaching. Year after year he led the child into the woods because he wanted his child to experience the thrills he had experienced in the woods. One day as they were walking the paths they had traveled through the woods so many times before, the veteran hunter realized that the child was slowly, patiently, quietly leading and he (the teacher) was doing the following.

I walk more slowly as I consider how that particular illustration touched me during the service last Sunday night. My son was telling the story, and his teenage daughter was sitting beside me. I suddenly realized that his deer story was also our story. He had become the leader, and I the follower. Soon his illustration will become his story as well. His daughter will lead, and he will follow.

If our lives for Christ mean anything, then at some point in our relationship with the Lord we should be able to look around us and see those we once led doing the leading. I also realize that because someone is trying to follow us, we must walk a path they can follow. I am reminded of Paul who encouraged his listeners to be like him as he was like Christ (see 1 Cor. 4:16). I think of times when I must walk more slowly, more patiently, and more lovingly so that those around me might be able to follow. I thank God for those who have walked ahead of me and helped me grow into a person who can also lead others.

PRAYER FOR TODAY

Help me lead in such a way that those who follow may grow into those who lead.

Follow my example as I follow the example of Christ.
—1 Corinthians 11:1

ADDITIONAL SCRIPTURE READING
Philippians 3:17; 1 Timothy 4:12, 16; Titus 2:7; 1 Peter 2:21

"It is no use walking anywhere to preach
unless our walking is our preaching."

—ST. FRANCIS OF ASSISI (1182–1226), Italian religious leader

≥ 8 ≤

I FELL TODAY

I FELL TODAY. I really didn't hurt myself too much, but it was a shock. Strolling along as usual, I stumbled and fell on the blacktop before I could catch myself.

Just yesterday, I had thought about what I would do if I fell while I was walking. I had given myself several options. One was to lie still and check myself for injury. Another was to wait until someone came along to help me up, but I quickly discarded that idea because I often walk for an hour and no one passes by. When I actually fell, I found myself so surprised and jolted that for a few minutes I did nothing. Then I began to check the damage—a scraped knee with some gravel embedded in the wound. It was nothing that wouldn't heal quickly. In a few weeks, there would be no permanent evidence of my fall.

As I rose slowly to my feet, I began searching for what had caused my fall. Nothing was evident. How could I have fallen on such a familiar path? What could have caused me to stumble? I had walked this way so often. Whatever the cause, I now had a small reminder that even on the most familiar pathways we can sometimes fall.

My fall is so very like my Christian life. Usually I find I have fallen in the most familiar circumstances. Many times I am not seriously injured, but the wound is there, and I am always a bit shaken to discover I am down.

Daily Bible study, for example, is a familiar environment in which I find myself falling down. I read my Bible, I search the Scriptures when I have a question or a lesson to prepare, but frequently I realize I have not opened my Bible for several days. I am easily distracted, and soon I am down. Another stumbling point for me is prayer. After a fall, I search and at first find no obvious reason for it, but suddenly I realize my prayer life is lacking. I have a small scrape with little pebbles of worry and discouragement embedded in my heart. I begin to pray again, and the scrape begins to heal.

Each day scrapes from discontent, impatience, and unconcern chafe my soul and leave their wound. But the wonderful part of all of this is that they heal because of Jesus. Again and again he heals me. Whenever I fall, I can get up and walk again knowing that the scrape will heal and the scar will fade because of his death on the cross for me.

PRAYER FOR TODAY

Lord, help me to remember that even when I fall, you are there to pick me up and heal my scrapes. Help me to be more observant in my daily devotional walk so that I don't stumble and fall in familiar territory. Most of all Lord thank you for your Son who took away my sins.

If the LORD delights in a man's way, he makes his steps firm; though he stumble, he will not fall, for the LORD upholds him with his hand.
—Psalm 37:23, 24

ADDITIONAL SCRIPTURE READING
Psalm 55:22

> "Often faltering feet come surest to the goal."
> —HENRY VAN DYKE (1852–1933), *Reliance*

PEOPLE PASSING BY

T HE ROAD I walk each day is just a country blacktop, so the traffic isn't too heavy between 6:00 a.m. and 8:00 a.m. Usually the same cars and the same drivers pass by me each morning. I meet them all—the old farmer on his way to drink coffee with his fellow farmers at the local restaurant, the teenage athlete headed for early basketball practice, the dedicated older gentleman who has spent the night with a sick friend (he goes every night at 8 o'clock and comes home every morning at 6:30), the young mother delivering her two small children to the sitter as she heads for her job at the bank in town, and now and then a hunter when squirrels or deer are in season.

Most of these people travel the same road, at the same time every morning. If I don't meet one of them for a morning or two, I become concerned. They have the same response to my journey. They expect me to walk that route at that time each day. If for some reason I am not walking along the road to the bridge, they become concerned and check with each other about me. Even though none of them are walkers, they want to know that I walk each day.

I had been negligent about my walking for a few days, and just last night one of these people telephoned and asked about my absence. As I wave to him during my walk this morning, I consider the similarities to my spiritual life.

The people I meet on a daily basis expect me to walk like Christ. Neighbors and friends may know I say I am a Christian, but saying it and doing it are not the same. If I really want them to believe it, I must *walk the talk* every day. Just as they observe when I am lax about my physical walking, they even more readily recognize my failure in my spiritual walking.

The much-used phrase—*we're the only Bible some people will ever read*—reminds me that my actions may be all the knowledge of Jesus others have. Although some of my friends and the people I meet are not Christians, they know I am. Like the fellow travelers who share my morning route, my fellow travelers in life have the same expectation. They expect to see me walking the Christian way. So I come to the end of my daily physical journey and realize once again that it isn't the big, outstanding events of life that win most people to Christ; the best testimony is found in how we walk the daily road.

PRAYER FOR TODAY

God help me to walk in such a way that the people I meet might be drawn to a closer relationship with you. Help my daily walk to reflect the love of you and your Son.

Whatever happens, conduct yourselves in a
manner worthy of the gospel of Christ.
—Philippians 1:27

ADDITIONAL SCRIPTURE READING

Deuteronomy 11:19; Psalm 89:15; Colossians 3:17

DRESS PROPERLY

For walking comfort, dress in layers. Layers protect from cold or rain and can be removed easily for comfort. Avoid cotton fabric next to the body because it will hold moisture.

"Walking is the favorite sport of the good and wise."

—A. L. ROWSE, *The Use of History*

➤ 10 ⪡

JOY IN THE MORNING

I T RAINED LAST night! After days of record-breaking heat and humidity, the rain finally came. It came with a prelude of thunder and lightning, followed by a beautiful chorus of steady rain through the darkness of the night.

The earth rejoices as I walk this morning. Robins flap their wings in the puddles on the blacktop and sing a new song. The corn's green leaves that were rolled so tightly yesterday, as protection from the heat, are now spread wide. A big, black crow flies overhead celebrating with loud screams over the new, wet morning as the little squirrel scampers on the path below. Even the brown spots in the yard seem restored and ready to sprout a patch of new green grass. God is in his heaven. For now all is right with this piece of the world. I realize that the rest of the world is still there, but I am refreshed as the cool breeze caresses my skin. I am renewed by the morning sights and sounds brought by the rain that we have needed so desperately.

The dawn of this day reminds me of our worship service last Sunday. Our congregation has been scorched with grief. Our minister of twenty-seven years recently lost his battle with cancer, and we are dry and barren from the tears we have shed. This man's life had touched the lives of his congregation as well as many people in the world around him. His loss has left a bare spot in many lives. Our church family has curled into itself much like the leaves on the corn in order to survive this time of drought. Then, last Sunday, the drought was broken with the *rain* of music and youthful energy.

Two young adults our pastor had ministered to as children and teenagers came with a group of six other young adults to share with us God's Word in music. Just as the rain covered the ground this morning and refreshed the parched, dry earth, their music covered us with God's message of love and refreshed us. At last we sang and celebrated a new day. Our grief is still there, but we were touched and encouraged to take our burdens to the Lord. We were renewed to serve our Lord Jesus Christ who has done so much for us.

PRAYER FOR TODAY

Thank you Lord, for young people who are willing to share their talents so that your Word might be shared and your love be made known to the world. Thank you for families who have nourished and strengthened them, both physically and spiritually. Thank you for ministers and congregations that love and support children who use their God-given talents and become the adult servants you want them to be.

Weeping may remain for a night, but rejoicing comes in the morning.
—Psalms 30:5

ADDITIONAL SCRIPTURE READING
Revelation 7:17; 21:4

WALKING SAFETY

- Keep safety in mind when you plan your route.
- Walk in the daytime or at night in well-lighted areas.
- Walk facing traffic.
- Do not wear headphones.
- Be aware of your surroundings.

≥ 11 ∈

SPIDER WEBS

AS I STEP outside my front door, I walk into a spider web. It stretches across my face like a mask at Halloween. I detest the sticky, creepy feeling. I reach to wipe it from my skin. In the early morning fog, I see spider webs are everywhere—on the grass, on the fence, even in the branches of the trees. The droplets of dew highlight each one, and then the sun slides through the fog and illuminates each masterpiece! I stop in awe and gaze at the webs that had been such a bother to me a few moments before. I see the promises of God.

I walk in the beauty of God's world as the sun makes rainbows in the spider webs. The intricate, thin thread spun into each individual, lacy pattern reminds me that I am God's unique creation. His beloved child! He knows the number of hairs on my head and promises me he will take care of me if I will let the light of his Son shine through the fog of my life. Just as the sun coming through the fog turned spider webs into works of beautiful, shimmering, woven lace, so can I be beautiful to God.

Too often I let the fog of worry and the fatigue of everyday concerns engulf me. As I let the entanglement with the spider web obliterate the beauty around me, I also let the concerns of life keep me from the beauty God has prepared for my life as his child. I could be the witness he intends for me to be here on earth if I would let the light of his love create rainbows in my daily life. Clinging to God, my life could be like the sun reflecting through the damp spider webs clinging to the fence—a thing of beauty.

The problems in my life become so like the spider webs across my face—clinging and sticking to me as I, by myself, try to wipe them away. Jesus told us, "Do not worry about your life. Look at the birds of the air; they do not sow or reap or store away in barns, and yet your heavenly Father feeds them. Are you not much more valuable than they . . . And why do you worry about clothes? See how the lilies of the field grow. They do not labor or spin. Yet I tell you that not even Solomon in all his splendor was dressed like one of these" (Matt. 6:25–29).

And then he tells us what I so often forget, "But seek first his kingdom and his righteousness, and all these things will be given to you as well" (Matt. 6:33).

PRAYER FOR TODAY

Lord, help me to remember the words of the psalmist "O Lord, our Lord, How majestic is your name in all the earth" and to "seek first his kingdom, and his righteousness." Keep me from being so concerned about the things of the world that my mind forgets the things of the kingdom.

> *O Lord, our Lord, how majestic is your name in all the earth . . .*
> *When I consider your heavens, the work of your fingers . . .*
> *what is man that you are mindful of him?*
> —Psalm 8:1–4

ADDITIONAL SCRIPTURE READING
Matthew 6:25–34

SHOES

Walking shoes must fit properly, so an experienced shoe salesperson should assist you when you shop for shoes. Often an athletic shoe store is the best place to purchase new walking shoes. Once you have been fitted properly for your first pair, you may be able to purchase shoes at a less-expensive location.

≥ 12 ≤

A COLD, RAINY DAY

IT IS COLD and cloudy today. Not bone-biting cold, just damp and chilly, typical November weather for Illinois. I really don't want to walk today. I don't have to answer to anyone about whether I walk or not, and today I just don't feel like it. With my attitude, I'm not sure it would do me any good anyway. There will be other days to walk when the sun is shining, and I am in a better mood. Besides, I will have to get my sweatpants out and put on that dumb-looking stocking cap, and I don't even know where it is. I finally find my cap and gloves a short time after lunch. (I had procrastinated because of more "important" duties.) I force myself to put on the ugly, bright orange stocking cap and the *flattering* black sweatpants. I do not intend to walk my normal route; however, once I begin, there seems to be no reason to defer from business as usual.

How very glad I am that I did walk. My mood changed much like the season around me. The beauty in the dark clouds overhead thrilled me. The dry corn stalks reminded me of the bountiful, safe harvest we have just finished. I thought of my deer-hunter son and how happy he would be to sit in the woods with his bow on this dreary day. I prayed for our soon-to-be granddaughter in Romania. Today is the day she will no longer be a ward of the government of Romania so the adoption proceedings can now begin! I thanked God for my adult children, their families and their faith. Despite the negative attitude with which I began my walk, I returned to the house uplifted and ready to work at the tasks before me.

I have had similar experiences with going to church services. At times, I really don't want to go. I am ill prepared and it seems such an effort to get ready. I don't have the proper attitude. I tell myself that whether or not I go isn't anyone's business but mine. I convince myself that no one would really miss me anyway so what would it matter if I didn't go one time? But I go to church anyway, just as I walked, and each time I come home blessed and thankful that I hadn't missed that particular service.

PRAYER FOR TODAY

Thank you Lord for making me realize that even if I'm not in the mood or haven't prepared, you have arranged special things for me each day and at each worship service. Help me remember that these activities are for my benefit and that it is a privilege to walk and to worship.

Let us not give up meeting together, as some are in the habit of doing.
—Hebrews 10:25

ADDITIONAL SCRIPTURE READING
Acts 2:42–47; 20:7; 1 Corinthians 16:2

WALKING FOR HEALTH
The most important thing is simply to set aside part of each day and walk. No matter what your age or condition, it's a practice that can make you healthier and happier.

—Courtesy of the President's Council on Physical Fitness and Sports

"Walking is good for the soul."

—ANDREW W. ROONEY, "Walking with Horse in Hand," *Word for Word*

⇒ 13 ⇐

ROBIN IN THE SNOW

T HE SNOW IS beautiful this morning. Sparkling rainbows shimmer on the snow as the sun reflects from the snow-covered branches of our big maple tree. My breath makes a white cloud trail as I shuffle up the driveway. I am so engrossed in the beauty around me that I almost miss the little bird hunched under the tree, but I slide to a stop and observe this phenomenon. We have not had any temperatures above freezing for some time, yet here in my backyard is a robin.

Carefully choosing my footsteps, I creep toward a full-grown, red-breasted robin. There it sits in the snow—cold, alone, and quite out of place. It appears to be frozen to this particular spot. As I reach out to help, a shudder of wings and tail feathers are its only signs of life. Stretching my gloved hand slowly toward its orange breast, I cup my hand under its body and gradually pull it loose from the thin layer of ice that has formed around its tiny feet. It cuddles for a moment in the warmth of my glove, then flutters its eyes, flaps its wings, and flies away. I stand amazed.

The image of the robin stays in my mind most of the day. As I compare the robin in the snow to my life in the world, I realize that I too get caught in the cold of the world. I find myself stuck in a situation or circumstance from which I can't get free. I wonder what I'm doing there. Often I have walked into these sticky, cold circumstances because I haven't been paying attention. Once I realize where I am and what has happened, I can't get myself out.

Conversations that aren't appropriate for Christians would be one of those spots—gossipy, backbiting, hateful conversations that freeze out any sign of Christ's love. Time and again I find myself stuck in a discussion that I don't want to be in, yet don't know how to escape.

An attitude of ingratitude is also a *cold* spot in my life. I get stuck in days of—*why me Lord?*—when I refuse to consider all of God's goodness toward me. I catch myself listing everything that is wrong with my husband, my children, my friends, and anyone else who happens to cross my path that day. I know that what I am doing is wrong, but I can't seem to escape the cutting, bitter attitude I have drifted into.

On such days I must remind myself that Jesus has reached down and rescued me from my own actions. Much like the robin, I have been set free. I can warm myself in his loving hands and fly free to serve him in the world around me.

PRAYER FOR TODAY

Lord, keep me from getting stuck in situations in the world that I really shouldn't be in in the first place. Help me to stay away from these temptations more each day. I stand amazed that you could love me. Thank you for Jesus and what he did for me on the cross.

Let your conversation be always full of grace, seasoned with salt,
so that you may know how to answer everyone.
—Colossians 4:6

ADDITIONAL SCRIPTURE READING
Matthew 6:12, 16:26; John 15:19; 17:14;
2 Corinthians 10:3

"Do not go where the path may lead, go instead
where there is no path and leave a trail."

—RALPH WALDO EMERSON (1803–1882), author and essayist

⇒ 14 ⇐

MALL WALKING

IT IS BITTER COLD and the weather reporters are predicting more snow mixed with rain, so I decide to head for the indoor mall. Mall walking always delights me. Walking and shopping are two of my favorite activities, and when I can do both at once, it is an added blessing.

When I enter the mall, my adrenaline starts flowing. I realize that I am not going to be walking alone. Many dedicated walkers are mingling with dedicated shoppers. Exhilarated, I join the crowd.

I launch my exercise regime by walking briskly so that I can finish my serious walking and get on with the fun part of the day. WINTER SALE signs in the windows immediately distract me, however, and I slow to a shopping stroll. Then my shopping mode kicks in, and for the next two hours I find myself touching, testing, and, of course—buying. Suddenly, it is time to go. I had come specifically to walk, but how easily the surrounding *things* distracted me. Although I knew that diversion was a possibility when I entered the mall, I really felt I could successfully walk *and* shop. Apparently my desire to walk is not as strong as I thought. I should have stayed with my outdoor walking routine.

I have had similar experiences in my spiritual life. I am serious about growing in the Lord. I want to study and learn from his Word. I make plans for a daily Bible study. I begin a Scripture-memorization program. I join a group of fellow Christians for fellowship and to strengthen my accountability. My enthusiasm is high. Then, reality hits.

I am invited for a day of shopping on the same day as my Bible study, and I go shopping. Thinking I will resume my schedule the next day, I skip one day's memorization for a quick cup of coffee with a friend. My fellowship group decides to meet on the same night as my bridge club, so just once, I choose to play bridge. My enthusiasm for spiritual growth wanes. I know what God expects and plan to do it, but the things around me so easily distract me. Just like my mall walking experience, I think I can do it all, but the truth is I must establish priorities. I need to go back to my original plan and stay with it.

PRAYER FOR TODAY

Keep me from being distracted by the things of the world Lord. Help me to realize that even though my desires may not be evil, they can keep me from growing in you. Help me to put first things first. I want to be your servant.

But seek his kingdom, and these things will be given to you as well.
—Luke 12:31

ADDITIONAL SCRIPTURE READING
Luke 12:32–34; Matthew 6:21

"We are under-exercised as a nation. We look, instead of play. We ride instead of walk. Our existence deprives us of the minimum of physical activity essential for healthy living."
—PRESIDENT JOHN F. KENNEDY

TRASH IN THE DITCH

WHEN I WALKED Sunday morning, the ground was covered with a mantle of clean, white snow and the world around me was fresh and pure. As the day went on, the sun warmed the earth, and the pristine environment of the morning melted into mud puddles and dead grass. Now it is Monday. The ditches are full of muddy water, and the trash is strewn across clumps of muddy grass. I look at the refuse in the roadside ditch—crushed soda and beer cans—the McDonald's bag with yesterday's soggy fries—all remnants of our throwaway society. What a mess! What a sad reflection of our attitude toward God's creation. I suppose the trash had been there yesterday, but the blanket of white snow had hidden the filth so evident today.

As I reflect on the ugliness of the scene before me, I am reminded of my sins and how they must look to God. My petty lies, my unlovely attitude toward my neighbor, my gossip of the day before, my pride in my own accomplishments, my selfish desires for my family, my lack of love for God—all are like the refuse in the ditch. How he must hate the ugly dregs of daily living that remain after the day is gone. I recognize anew the truly awesome gift Christ gave me when he died on the cross.

Because I have Jesus as my Savior, he covers all those ugly sins with his blood. He makes them "white as snow." When God looks at me, he looks through the eyes of my Savior, and all the nasty rubbish of my life appears pure and spotless.

What a beautiful thought for today. Jesus covers my sins much like the snow covers the filth in the ditches along my road. As I continue my walk, I remind myself that these things of life I find so appealing are just throwaway items like the trash in the ditch. Jesus will take all the garbage of my life and make it new in God's eyes.

PRAYER FOR TODAY

Thank you, Lord, for Jesus and his death on the cross. Thank you for sending your Son that I might have forgiveness for the rubbish in my life even though I know I don't deserve it. Thank you for your goodness.

Wash me, and I will be whiter than snow.
—Psalm 51:7

ADDITIONAL SCRIPTURE READING
Isaiah 1:18

"The speed at which you walk is less important than the time you devote to it, although it is recommended that you walk as briskly as your condition permits. It takes about twenty minutes for your body to begin realizing the 'training effects' of sustained exercise. The talk test can help you find the right pace. You should be able to carry on a conversation while walking. If you're too breathless to talk, you're going too fast."

—Courtesy of The President's Council on Physical Fitness and Sports

⇒ 16 ⇐

THE SECOND MILE

D URING MY EARLY morning walks, I often specu-
late about how my route and attitude toward that
route are much like my Christian life. Although
my scenery may be different and the road may be smooth or rocky, my
attitude is the same.

The first mile is great. I feel good, the path is smooth, my anticipation is high. The struggle begins in the second mile when it starts
to be an uphill course. My legs begin to get tired, my breathing
becomes more difficult, my desire and anticipation have dwindled. I
begin to wonder why I thought this method of exercise was such a
good idea! Just putting one foot in front of the other in order to reach
the top of the hill is my only goal.

I keep plodding, looking neither to the left nor right, but only
toward the top of the hill on the horizon. Just when I feel my breath
is gone and my legs will hold me no longer, I reach the summit. I
have made it! Adrenaline starts flowing; my feet quit dragging; my
heart stops pounding. As I head down the hill, I have things under
control again. I am almost at the end of my walk. I'm headed home.

For many of us, living for Christ is like this. Many of us start with
fervor and anticipation only to find themelves slowing down as we get
into it. Satan begins to put up roadblocks. An old temptation raises
its ugly head. A fellow Christian disappoints us. Grim reality hits.
Death and loss are still with us. Grief slows us down. Life for a time
becomes nothing more than putting one foot in front of the other.

We often bring our second-mile situations of life to the Lord's
Table. It is here we nourish our souls so that we might have the

strength to walk the *second miles* in our life. We find we can join the apostle Paul in saying, "I can do everything through him who gives me strength" (Phil. 4:13). With this renewed strength, we can continue to plod or, perhaps, "to mount up with wings as eagles" until we reach the top of the hill and start that last part of our journey home.

PRAYER FOR TODAY

While I am at your table Lord, heal my second-mile hurts. Give me the strength to do what you have for me to do today. May I, too, die to my old self and walk on as a new person in Christ who looks to you for guidance in all things.

I can do everything through him who gives me strength.
—Philippians 4:13

ADDITIONAL SCRIPTURE READING
Isaiah 40:31; Matthew 11:28

"Climb the mountains and get their good tidings.
Nature's peace will flow into you as sunshine flows into trees.
The winds will blow their own freshness into you and
the storms their energy, while cares will drop off like autumn
leaves. As age comes on, one source of enjoyment after
another is closed, but nature's sources never fail."

—JOHN MUIR (*Our National Parks*,
Houghton, Mifflin and Company, 1901)

⇒ 17 ⇐

I QUIT!

I HAVE QUIT WALKING! I really don't know how it happened. One morning, when it was raining, I didn't want to use the treadmill in the basement, so I just didn't walk. I thought one morning wouldn't matter. Although I thought about walking several times later that day, it just wasn't convenient. The next morning I postponed my walk because I was waiting for an important phone call. I don't even remember what excuse I had for the next day or the next, but just this morning I realized it has been almost a month since that first rainy morning! I haven't walked for almost a month!

After the first few days, it became easier to find excuses. Phone calls, weather, work, and aching muscles seemed to be such legitimate reasons at the time. Now I'm a little stiffer than when I walked each day, but not too much. I'm not quite as energetic either, but my energy level fluctuates now that I am getting "older." I am not as "up" emotionally, but no one seems to notice. The change has been so gradual, but today I recognize the reason for my low-down physical and mental attitude: I quit walking! I immediately put on my shoes and sweatshirt and head off down the road!

At times, I quit walking spiritually with much the same results. Involvement in the journey of daily living can distract me from my spiritual walking, and I experience similar results. It happens so gradually that I hardly realize what I have done. Then suddenly, like my experience today with walking, I wonder why I am so "low-down." I acknowledge to myself and to the Lord that I have quit "walking." I pick up my Bible and go to the Lord in prayer!

PRAYER FOR TODAY

Lord, I want to be consistent in my walk with you. I don't want to make excuses and be too busy to complete the exercises that keep me spiritually fit and close to you. Remind me how easy it is to quit walking. Keep me on your road.

O that my ways were steadfast.
—Psalms 119:5

ADDITIONAL SCRIPTURE READING

Isaiah 7:9; Galatians 5:1; James 5:8

"If you would attain to what you are not yet, you must always be displeased by what you are. For where you are pleased with yourself there you have remained. Keep adding, keep walking, keep advancing."

—SAINT AUGUSTINE (*The Confessions,* AD 697)

≥ 18 ≤

MUSHROOM TIME

I T IS MUSHROOM TIME! An early spring shower and some hot sunshine for more than a day always lure the mushroom hunters to the woods. I notice my neighbor's old pickup truck parked beside the woods early in the morning, then I see two other familiar vehicles from the local village. I know the hunt has begun in force. Serious hunters have a private cove, a rotting log, or wooded nook that is their own secret spot. I, too, am captivated by the excitement of searching for the mysterious morels and wander into the woods for a hasty hunting expedition.

Head down, I shuffle through the damp, dead leaves of last fall hoping against hope that I might stumble onto the spongelike cones that suddenly appear overnight. I know to be careful that I find the real thing and not the false morels that can cause sickness or even death. Many people, in their eagerness to find the biggest or the most, have been fooled by these "look-alikes" of nature. My son and grandson can quickly discern between the good and the poisonous, but I am not as familiar with the miniscule differences in the two plants.

I scuff along slowly, searching beneath the leaves of the mayapple plants with the aid of a small, fallen branch. I listen to the chatter of the squirrels as I invade their territory. Shadows and rays of sunlight play across my path. As I step around a decaying log, I see it: an enormous yellow sponge—the best kind. I quickly find another and another—I have found my own patch. I drop to my knees, gathering the delicacies into the folded tails of my shirt. Plopping to sit on the damp ground, I begin to examine my stash. I must have thirty or more beautiful sponge mushrooms. What a find! I can't wait to tell my family.

I leave the woods and head home. As I walk, I think about the mushrooms in my shirttail knapsack. I suppose they are the real things. They look the same as those my friends bring home. They were growing in the right kind of environment. Yet doubts regarding my good fortune start to form. I really don't have enough knowledge to be absolutely sure these mushrooms are good for us. I could seriously endanger my family. The farther I walk, the more I worry.

When I arrive home, I decide to make sure I have the real thing. I'll ask some questions. I'll look at pictures on the Internet. I'll find people who really know. I deposit them in the basket by the door and go to the phone, determined to find answers before I feed them to my family.

Later, sitting in my lawn chair with coffee in hand, I realize I need to exercise the same discernment in relationship to Christian people. So many people can appear to be "the real thing." They are in the right environment. They do and say everything that is expected, yet I need to test what they say. I need to become knowledgeable about God's Word to be sure that what I hear and see is truly of God. It is easy to become excited about a message because of how good it sounds, or because I really want to believe it. Yet, I must be cautious. I need to examine everything I share with my family and friends to be certain that it is the complete truth.

Even more important than testing other people, I need to test my own actions, speech, and environment. Paul tells us in 1 Thessalonians 5:21, 22: "Test everything. Hold on to the good. Avoid every kind of evil." I must be very careful that I am walking and talking in such a way that I don't cause those I feed spiritually to become ill.

PRAYER FOR TODAY

Lord, my prayer today is that those with whom I come in contact can test me and find me to be "the real thing" as a Christian. I pray that I will study your Word so I might recognize truth and reject evil.

Test everything. Hold on to the good. Avoid every kind of evil.
—1 Thessalonians 5:21, 22

ADDITIONAL SCRIPTURE READING

1 Thessalonians 5

"Every problem has a gift for you in its hands."

—RICHARD DAVID BACH (b. 1936),

American author, *Jonathan Livingston Seagull*

⇒ 19 ⇐

THE ROBIN'S NEST

FOR SEVERAL MORNINGS I have been watching a pair of robins build a nest in the old maple tree beside my driveway. The first morning I noticed a little red string in the bird's mouth. As I stopped to watch, the robin flew to a low branch of the maple tree and carefully deposited the treasure on what appeared to be an insignificant stack of twigs. When I returned from my walk, I hesitated beneath the branches, but saw no sign of the robins or their creation.

The next morning as I started out the driveway, I could see the robins' progress. Barely visible through the budding leaves I could see a dark shadow area highlighted by a bright red string! As I watched, one and then the other robin flew in carrying small bits of dry grass and remnants of last autumn's leaves. They carefully placed their contribution and quickly departed to the nearby yard and fields for more building material. Patiently and persistently they continued. Again and again they flew in, left their material, and departed.

Each morning since, I have checked their progress. This morning I saw the completed nest—a beautiful example of persistence and patience. I lingered for a moment just admiring their creation, then thought of God's great wisdom in His creation and how so often the simplest rituals of nature remind me of attributes I need in my own life. This week, a reminder of patience and persistence was just what I needed.

I want so many things to happen now—not later. I become so impatient and want the young boy in my Sunday school class to accept Christ this very day rather than patiently and persistently teaching him and guiding him into the love of Christ. I fear that my impatience with some of my young women friends is much too obvious. If only I could show them more patience as they struggle to juggle husbands, jobs, children, and church. Paul tells me in Titus 2:4 that the older women are to teach the younger. I attempt to be an example and a teacher to younger women, but I want them to instantly understand the appropriate priorities in a Christian woman's life. So many times I must go to my Lord and ask not only for patience but for forgiveness for my impatience with his children.

Even worse is my impatience with my Lord and his plan for me and for his kingdom. I believe "in all things God works for the good of those who love him" (Rom. 8:28), but I find myself sometimes asking: *Why not now, God?* Repeatedly, I must go back, like the robins, and patiently, persistently continue to build what God has given me to build, whether it is a small boy's spiritual growth, a young mother's spiritual maturity, or just my own daily walk with the Lord.

PRAYER FOR TODAY

God, remind me that patience with my fellow Christians is a fruit of the spirit that I need to portray to those around me. Help me to grow in this area of my life so that those around me might better understand your patience and your love. I thank you for the strength I gain from coming to you for the qualities I need on a daily basis.

Warn those who are idle, encourage the timid, help the weak, be patient with everyone.
—1 Thessalonians 5:14

ADDITIONAL SCRIPTURE READING
Proverbs 14:29; 19:11; 1 Corinthians 13:4; Titus 2:4

"There is no road too long to the man who advances deliberately and without undue haste; there are no honors too distant to the man who prepares himself for them with patience."

—JEAN DE LA BRUYÈRE (1645–96), French writer and moralist

⇛ 20 ⇚

FLIGHT FROM THE NEST

I WATCHED THE robins build their nest earlier this spring and daily have inspected the three blue eggs inside the nest. One day three naked, squirming bodies replaced the eggs. Bright orange little mouths popped open each time I nudged the nest. I backed away quickly and smiled as Mother Robin swooped in with her early morning worm. The little ones clamored for her attention as she deposited her find, and then she flew off to continue her breakfast scavenges.

I passed by each morning for several weeks to check the nest for progress. Mother Robin is doing her job well. Her babies have feathered out quite nicely. Then this morning I spy one teetering on the edge of the nest. The mother is perched on a branch quite close to the nest. She seems to be almost hovering over her young chick. I wonder if she realizes that soon all three will be gone and her work will be finished.

Walking on, I think about how difficult it is to watch your fledglings fly. Each "flight" our children make is important for their growth, yet, as it appeared to be for Mother Robin, it is difficult to let them spread their wings. Our children leave home for a few hours, then for a few days, and sooner than we would like they spread their wings and fly off with a mate and children of their own. God has given us humans more time than the creatures of the animal kingdom to train our children for flight, and that time is so very important.

The writer of Proverbs tells us to "train a child in the way he should go, and when he is old he will not turn from it" (Prov. 22:6). Children are a special gift from God, and it is our responsibility as parents to raise them for him. Training is not easy. God's way often is not the way of the world, so teaching a child to *fly* in today's social environment becomes a difficult task. Whether the children we teach are our own or someone else's, they should see us flying under God's wing. Just as the baby bird watched its mother's flight pattern, so do our children imitate our pattern.

I have heard my daughter, and in later years my granddaughters, say or do something that I know came directly from me—my mouth or my actions. Sometimes I have been proud of their imitation, but in other instances it has caused me to examine my speech and attitudes. Often our adult children make decisions that exemplify the pattern we followed throughout their childhood. One of the most important patterns to teach our children is to put God first. When Jesus was asked what the most important commandment is, he answered, "Love the Lord your God with all your heart and with all your soul and with all your mind and with all your strength. The second is this: 'Love your neighbor as yourself'" (Mark 12:30, 31). If only we could ingrain this thought into our young people, they would be prepared to *fly* in any situation.

As I walk down the road toward home, I smile to myself that these thoughts came only by watching a little robin on the edge of the nest. When I pass back by the nest, the little bird is gone. Apparently he has left the nest as all our young ones do. I hope he is prepared.

PRAYER FOR TODAY

Thank you for my children, Lord. I pray that I have taught them as you would have them taught, and that I can be an example to young people whether they are my grandchildren or someone else's. I pray that more of the children of the world may be taught about your love and your son Jesus, and what he has done for all of us.

Train up a child in the way he should go
—Proverbs 22:6

ADDITIONAL SCRIPTURE READING

Deuteronomy 4:9; Proverbs 17:6; Mark 12:30; Acts 2:39

"If you love someone, set them free. If they come back they're yours; if they don't they never were."

—RICHARD BACH, American author, *Jonathan Livingston Seagull*

⇒ 21 ⇐

ADOPTED IN LOVE

EVERY TIME I walk, I see God's plan for nature in action around me. Today, in the field across the road, little lambs are playing close to their mothers' sides. A newborn calf scrambles to find his momma's milk. Babies are calling for their mothers; mothers are nurturing and feeding their young ones. As I admire this spring ritual, a stray white-faced Hereford calf searching for its mother wanders into the picture. He stumbles across the uneven ground to where a rather scrawny little newborn calf is nursing at the side of his big, Black Angus mother. Fascinated, I watch the scene unfold. The intruder edges up to the mother and her nursing baby and gently nudges the scrawny calf sucking at its mother. Nothing happens. The stranger nudges harder, but still no response from the newborn. Momma turns, notices the newcomer, and positions herself so that both might nurse at her side. It is apparent that she has adopted the orphan. Because I am familiar with the ways of the farm, I know that both of these babies will depend on that cow as long as they need her nourishment.

I continue my walk and think about the behavior I have just witnessed. Adoption in our family is alive and well. I have an adopted niece, an adopted nephew, and two adopted grandchildren. How special and wonderful is each of these children in our family. They are as our own children and are treated no differently than birth children. All are our children.

To God, I am just like that. I am his adopted child. It matters not who I was before, where I have been, or what my nationality is. I am his child, and he will love me, nourish me, and protect me just as he did his own Son. How exciting it is to remember that I am a child of God! Paul, in his letter to the Galatians writes, "since you are a son, God has made you also an heir" (Gal. 4:7). Just as our grandchildren inherit equally with each other, I, too, will inherit and can claim all of God's promises. Because of the love of my heavenly brother, Jesus Christ, I can inherit that most precious gift of all—eternal life with my heavenly Father. In Ephesians 1:5 Paul again speaks of adoption: "In love he predestined us to be adopted as his sons through Jesus Christ, in accordance with his pleasure and will." I like the "in accordance with his pleasure and will" phrase, as that is exactly the feeling I have about my grandchildren. It is such a blessing to know that God feels the same way about me!

PRAYER FOR TODAY

Heavenly Father, I love being adopted by you. Thank you for allowing me to be a part of your family here on earth, and most of all, I thank you for surrendering Jesus to die that I might live with you forever.

> *In love he predestined us to be adopted as his sons through Jesus Christ, in accordance with his pleasure and will.*
> —Ephesians 1:5

ADDITIONAL SCRIPTURE READING
Galatians 4:7; Romans 8:17

WALKING WITH CHILDREN

Scheduling a regular family walk is a great way to pass on healthy habits to your children. Spend time together and get fit at the same time.

⇒ 22 ⇐

PROMISES OF APRIL

THE CLOUDS OF my childhood fade as I stand by the grave of my father and watch the clods fall on the lid of the casket we had chosen. Only a few months ago I had watched him roll his wheelchair into the tunnel that would take him to board the plane for Florida. His body had finally worn out. The fight to survive was over. He turned, waved, and whispered, "See you in April." He was going back to die in the place he loved the most. He knew it. I knew it.

Now it is October. As I stand with my children and grandchildren in the October sunlight, I realize that my childhood is over—not in years, of course, but in my mind. As long as Dad was living, I had been a child. Now he is gone, and so is the child I had been. But the small part of me that always had been his child holds on to the phrase, "See you in April." As time goes by, I put it away; I bring it out; I grieve; I put it away; I bring it out; I grieve; I put it away; I bring it out. . . .

Icy fingers of grief keep cutting into my heart like bits of glass shattering on a marble surface. Cold, bone-piercing emotions penetrate the corners of my mind and lodge in the crevices of my thoughts. A winter of mourning stretches on and on, and cold grief becomes a part of me. Then the thawing flood of hope starts to seep into my heart. Warm, comforting tears bring the budding of hope in the dark, dingy caverns of sorrow. I keep hearing, "See you in April," and I know there must be a reason for this phrase.

Today, as I walk on this April morning, I finally see—I realize in my heart that April is a new birth. April is spring. In April, I celebrate my birthday. April represents all the good days I will yet have in life. April is my memories. April is the sure promise of a new life after the death of winter.

At last, I am able to say, "See you in April" and understand that we all are a part of God's plan. He has gone to prepare a place for us, and some day we will all celebrate April together. My grief isn't gone, but I can celebrate Easter, and April, and spring. See you in April, Dad.

PRAYER FOR TODAY

Remind me each day, Lord, that April is coming.

In my Father's house are many rooms, if it were not so, I would have told you. I am going there to prepare a place for you.
—John 14:2, 3

ADDITIONAL SCRIPTURE READING

2 Timothy 4:7, 8; Revelation 2:10

WALKING ROUTE

Don't avoid walking up hills; they make you stronger. If a hill is too steep for comfort, zigzag up or down.

≥ 23 ≤

HURT

TODAY I AM physically unable to walk, which is certainly a new experience for me. Yesterday, I wrecked our car. One of those unavoidable accidents that always happen to someone else happened to me. Because of the accident I find myself with a banged-up car, a banged-up knee, and a thankful heart.

My friend and the young man in the other car were not seriously injured, and for that I thank God. Even so, I see my friend's bruises and the pain of her fractured rib, and I feel a guilty sorrow that I caused her pain. I cannot remember ever having inflicted physical pain on anyone, other than a swat on the bottom for one of my children, and I am quite surprised by the sorrow it causes me. I have repeated how sorry I am over and over until my friend has told me to stop. Still, there is guilt within me that my actions could be the cause of her physical pain.

I sit here with my injured leg propped up on a stool and my new cane by my side for support, and I think and pray. I ask forgiveness for the times I have caused pain for those around me, especially pain that is not as obvious as a bruised knee but maybe more damaging. How often do we unintentionally cause pain to others with our words and actions? How often do we injure our Christian family or the reputation of a friend or neighbor by what we say—or by what we don't say?

Just as the auto accident happened in an instant, so can a harsh or angry word spoken do its damage. No matter how many times we say we are sorry, the word has been spoken, and the hurt is there. There may be the moment we could have spoken an encouraging word to a teenager but because of appearance, or language, or our own petty judgments, we let the moment pass, and the hurt is there; the scar remains. There are times when strangers enter our midst looking for acceptance, but we are so intent on our own world that we miss the moment to welcome them, and the hurt is there; the scar remains. I think of the unkind responses I have given to members of my own family—those I love the most—and ask God to forgive me for the scars I may have left on heart and soul.

As I continue this journey of life, I want to be aware of how quickly an accident can cause me to hurt not only myself, but also others in the world around me. More than that, I want to consciously be aware of the mental and spiritual hurt that can be caused by a careless or unkind word spoken in an instant of harsh feelings or, even worse, just not noticing or caring about the people around me.

PRAYER FOR TODAY

Lord, help me to remember that it takes only an instant to hurt those we love by our actions and our words. Help me to be aware that even though the injuries can heal, the scar is always there. Forgive me where I have caused pain and scars in the past with both my physical and spiritual actions.

A word aptly spoken is like apples of gold in settings of silver.
—Proverbs 25:11

ADDITIONAL SCRIPTURE READING
Proverbs 13:3; James 1:19; 2:3–12

"He who limps is still walking."

—J. LEC STANISLAW, Polish aphorist, poet, and satirist

⇥ 24 ⇤

ANNEKE IS HOME

I BEGIN MY WALK this morning, then stop to watch a
mother robin fly to her nest with "breakfast" for her little
ones. In the pasture, the newborn, white-faced Hereford
calves snuggle close to their mothers searching for their morning milk.
As I approach the pond, I hear the noisy quacking of a mother duck
summoning her ducklings to line up for a walk in the new spring
grass. All of nature is coming alive. It is spring in our part of the
world, and Anneke comes home today.

We have anticipated this homecoming for almost a year. Our
two-year-old adopted Romanian granddaughter will finally be at
home with her parents in America. Only we who are welcoming this
child know what a struggle her arrival has been. When Anneke was
eighteen months old, her birth mother took her to a Romanian
orphanage. Because Anneke was so healthy, the government orphanage asked her mother not to leave the little girl with them. The
orphanage supervisor suggested that the mother take her to S.E.E.K.
(an American organization) outside of Bucharest. The mother did,
and the process for this homecoming began. After many months of
paperwork and frustration, Anneke became our granddaughter. Today
we are celebrating the end of that process. Until six days ago, Anneke
had never heard a word of English. Now those of us who want to
squeeze her, touch her, and just look at her beautiful, wide-eyed little face surround her. Anneke is home!

As I hold this little one in my arms for the first time, I pray that
God will forgive my lack of faith. I did not discourage, but neither
did I encourage my daughter and her family in the decision to adopt

a child from another country. The horror stories of foreign adoption had continually filled my mind, and all of my prayers had been for my side of the situation. I am sorry to say that Anneke, the little girl who today (and for years to come) fills our family with such joy, was never really a part of my prayers. My prayers had been for my family and me.

How sad it is that we Christians are often this way. Even when God has a plan worked out for us, we continue to pray about our own worries and our own desires. As I look down at this little child snuggled in my arms, I truly see the smiling face of God and his plan for our family. I thank him for the faith of our adult children and his wisdom in knowing what is right for all of us. Once more, my faith in his wisdom has been increased.

PRAYER FOR TODAY

Lord, forgive me for my selfishness. Increase my faith. Remind me to pray that your will be done. Forgive me for not trusting you more in my day-to-day life. I know that you have a plan for my children and for me, as we are your children. Help me to trust you to work out that plan in your own way and your own time.

Trust in the Lord with all your heart and
lean not on your own understanding.
—Proverbs 3:5

ADDITIONAL SCRIPTURE READING

Psalm 33:11; Proverbs 16:3

"Never be afraid to trust an unknown future to a known God."

—CORRIE TEN BOOM, Dutch evangelist

≥ 25 ≤

DON'T YOU HEAR MUSIC?

I AM TRYING something different this morning—earphones and music. It is invigorating, and I know many people use them when they walk, but I don't think I will use them very often. I miss the sounds of the countryside around me. For the city dweller, the sound of the tractor in the distance, the barking dog, the cooing of the dove, and the hum of the locusts might sound dissonant, but in my ears they are soothing music. The sound in the earphones washes away the sounds around me and causes me to reminisce.

Several years ago, our young daughter sat in the back of the church entertaining a group of her peers with a song I had not heard before. When I asked her about it, she replied that she had written the song herself. I questioned her quite strongly because I thought she might be stretching the truth to impress her peers. She insisted that she had written the music herself and ended the conversation with what has now become a family statement: "Don't you hear music?" No one else in our family hears music. She has continued "hearing music" into her adult life and shares that music in praise to the Lord. It is her gift.

The little verse in the windowsill above my sink reads, "What we are is our gift from God. What we become is our gift to God." My immediate family and church family are filled with talented people—musicians, artists, seamstresses, and photographers. I have often said, "I really don't have any talents. I'm just here to appreciate the talents of others." I doubt that God is really pleased by that flippant statement. I don't think he wants me to belittle the talents he has given to me.

There are many different ways to "hear music" from God. I may not hear music, but I do have gifts. My problem is not that

God hasn't given me talents; but that I may not be listening for the "music" he has sent my way. Perhaps what I need to do is take another look at what God tells me in his Word. Paul wrote to the Romans, "We have different gifts, according to the grace given us" (Rom. 12:6). As I think about this, I know (if I am honest with myself) that words are my gift. Just as music is my daughter's gift, I have been given the ability to teach and write.

As I continue my walk, I reflect on what I am doing with that gift. Just yesterday I read Max Lucado's statement in *Applause from Heaven*: "There are things only you can do, and you are alive to do them. In the great orchestra we call life, you have an instrument and a song, and you owe it to God to play them both sublimely."

My song in life is writing and teaching, and I must get busy and sing my song to the best of my God-given ability.

PRAYER FOR TODAY

I praise you for all you have given me. Don't let me become "puffed up" or "think more highly" of myself than I should. Help me to remember that I am a part of your "orchestra" and that my "music" (whatever form it may take) is from you. I praise you for all you have given me. Help me Lord to use my gift that it may glorify you.

We have different gifts according to the grace given us.
—Romans 12:6

ADDITIONAL SCRIPTURE READING
1 Corinthians 12 and 13

"Use what talents you possess: the woods would be very silent if no birds sang there except those that sang best."

—HENRY VAN DYKE (1852–1933), clergyman and author

⇒ 26 ⇐

WALKING WITH WILLIE

I STAND AT THE end of my drive and wait for him to show up. As I anticipated, he wanders to the end of his road, looks both ways, sits down and waits. I walk toward him. He raises his head, stands up, wags his tail, and waits for me to reach him. Ever since he was a pup, Willie and I have walked together. He is my faithful friend on all my morning walks. My neighbors tell me he waits patiently for me every day even when I am on vacation.

I enjoy Willie's companionship. If there is danger along the way, he warns me with a low growl, a sudden stop, or a gruff bark. If he thinks I am walking too slowly, he circles me a couple of times, then nudges my hand with his nose. If I miss seeing a squirrel, a rabbit, or deer in the waterway, he is quick to point them out with a sharp yelp and a side trip to chase them in my direction. He often runs on ahead of me. Sometimes I lose sight of him, but I never doubt that he will return before we head home. When we return to Willie's road, he hesitates, and then turns toward his home. I know he'll be waiting tomorrow when we will walk again.

I sometimes wonder if I am as faithful a friend as Willie is. I wonder if my friends know I'll be there for them every time. Proverbs 17:17 tells us that a "friend loves at all times." A true friend walks with us every day and doesn't hesitate to warn us when we might be in a dangerous situation.

Sometimes, when I realize my friends may be headed for trouble emotionally or spiritually, I use those "it really isn't any of my business" or "I don't want to hurt their feelings" excuses and say nothing.

But just as Willie nudges me if I am not walking in the way he thinks I should, I should prod a friend who has slowed down spiritually. Yet, I hesitate to get too personal with someone else's spiritual life. After all, I tell myself, we aren't to judge others. These age-old excuses keep me from being the friend I should be. How important it is for me to remember what Paul writes in Colossians 3:16: "Let the word of Christ dwell in you richly as you teach and admonish one another with all wisdom." To be a faithful friend, I need to admonish with wisdom from God's Word.

One of the greatest pleasures in life are friends who want to share life's beauty and joy with those who are walking with them. My granddaughter phoned me at sunset the other day. As soon as I said "Hello," I heard, "Hey Gran, go outside. The sky is beautiful; I don't want you to miss it."

What a delight to glory in God's creation and share the joy with family and friends.

As I finish my walk for the day, I thank God for friends who have been faithful to me through the years. I thank him for those who have walked with me and have shared my heartaches and joys. I thank him for those who have had the courage to admonish me in wisdom and who have loved me at all times, even when I was unlovely.

PRAYER FOR TODAY

Help me, God, to be a faithful friend who loves at all times. Help me to know your Word that I might admonish with your wisdom and share your joy.

A friend loves at all times.
—Proverbs 17:17

ADDITIONAL SCRIPTURE READING

Proverbs 18:24; John 15:13; Colossians 3:16

"Don't walk in front of me, I may not follow. Don't walk behind me, I may not lead. Just walk beside me and be my friend."

—ALBERT CAMUS (1913–1960),

French existentialist, author, and philosopher

I MET LAUREN TODAY

EVEN THOUGH the figure walking toward me is just a shadow on the horizon, I know it is my granddaughter. Her slim silhouette with her ponytail swinging against the bright morning sky is a refreshing, familiar sight. Slowing my pace, I anticipate her response and am not disappointed. She lifts her head, smiles, quickly raises her arm in greeting, and increases her pace in my direction. We walk the same route, but we seldom walk together because I am an early riser and she is a teenager. As she approaches, her soft words—"Hey Gran! How ya doin'?"— touches the niche in my heart that only she can reach. This grandchild has lived at my back door her entire sixteen years. She is definitely my son's child in her response to the world around her. I see his actions and hear his words reflected in her so often. Even more awesome, I sometimes see myself in her.

We stop for a minute. She fills me in on her plans for the day, and I share with her the things I have experienced as I walked. I tell her about the deer in the waterway, the new mown hay, the little white flowers blooming at the edge of the woods, the buzzards flying overhead, the loose nails in the bridge planking—then we go on, each walking the same route but in different directions. She walks along the road I have just traveled, and I walk toward home. It suddenly strikes me how much our encounter parallels our Christian life.

My granddaughter is beginning her Christian walk with the Lord. I am finishing. Just as I share with her the physical experiences of my morning walk, I also share with her the experiences of my Christian walk. I want her to know the joy of the Lord. I want to help her recognize the beauty in a life for Christ. Just as I share about the little white flowers blooming by the woods, I also share the peace she will know if she takes Christ on her journey. Because I already have been down the road she is traveling, I warn her that there will be nails in her path. She will experience the pain of rejection, the sorrow of death, and the hurt of gossip. Sometimes the buzzards of the world will surround her. I need to assure her that the strength of her Lord and her family will be sufficient to support her along her path.

As I finish my morning walk, I thank God for the gift of this grandchild who I am bringing up in the nurture of the Lord. I thank him not only for her but also for all the strong, Christian teenagers who just want those of us who have walked before them to share the perils and joys of the road ahead.

PRAYER FOR TODAY

Lord, keep me on the right road. Help me to share the joys of walking with Christ with the young people in my family and in the world. Thank you for my children and their children. Make me a blessing in their lives.

Children's children are a crown to the aged.
—Proverbs 17:6

ADDITIONAL SCRIPTURE READING

Proverbs 22:6; 29:15, 17; Ephesians 6:4; Colossians 3:21

"To know the road ahead, ask those coming back."

—Chinese Proverb

≳ 28 ≲

PRAISE THE LORD!

SOME DAYS ARE just PRAISE THE LORD days! The teenagers came home from the Christ in Youth Conference singing "Our God Is An Awesome God," and if I knew all the words, that would be my song for the day. God *is* awesome!

The sun is shining; the humidity is gone, and it has quit raining. The simple silence of the countryside and the soft fragrance of the locust trees mingle with the pungent odor of wet hay as it begins to dry in the heat of the morning sun. My family is physically healthy, and more importantly, spiritually healthy. My grandchildren are the blessing God promised in Proverbs 17:7 that they would be. For now, all is well with my world.

As I walk this country road in Illinois, I pray for others on country roads and city sidewalks that they, too, might know the peace and presence of the Lord. I am aware that the many problems of the world are still there, and that much is wrong in society. I know that children are still hungry and people are still dying without Christ. I know tomorrow may bring heartache and worry, but right now, just for this moment, I can raise my voice with the psalmist and praise the Lord.

Because of minutes and sometimes days like today, I can face potentially difficult tomorrows. I know that God is in control no matter what may happen. I rejoice in the days when praising the Lord and appreciating the beauty and joy around me is enough for the moment. Today is one of those days!

PRAYER FOR TODAY

Thank you for a day such as today, Lord. I so need to remember who you are and who I am in you and that you really are in control of all things. You truly are an awesome God. I praise you today.

How awesome is the Lord Most High.
—Psalm 47:2

ADDITIONAL SCRIPTURE READING

Psalm 8; Psalm 121:1

"An early morning walk is a blessing for the whole day."
—HENRY DAVID THOREAU (Attributed)

⇒ 29 ⇐

EVERYONE KNOWS I WALK

ALMOST EVERYONE in my rural neighborhood knows I walk. Many times, folks I see in town or at a local business, greet me by saying, "How was walking today?" or "Well, how far today?" Some will make references to my friend Willie (the neighbor's dog) who walks with me. Others will comment about the hot or cold weather and how it must affect my walk. My walking is a way for them to initiate a conversation or make a personal comment. Many people comment that they know they should start some type of walking or exercise program too. I always respond by sharing how much better I feel and how much more energy I have when I maintain my daily walking regime. I have no problem sharing and encouraging them to begin to walk or to return to their exercise program. I am quite uninhibited in chatting about how good walking and exercise would be for them. After all, I do it every day and feel quite confident in sharing with them what walking has done for me.

I wish I had the same confidence in discussing my Christian walking. Most of my neighbors are aware that I attend church. I think most of them know I call myself a Christian, but very few asked me about it, and I seldom volunteer or bring Christ into my conversations. I certainly don't initiate conversations about my Lord in everyday, meet-on-the-street discussions.

Although I am recognized in our community as an outgoing, friendly individual, I find I can chat about the weather, the ballgame last night, the latest neighborhood news, or my walking program with much more confidence than I discuss Jesus and how much walking with him helps my daily life. Why is that? Why is it that I think only the professional Christians (preachers, etc.) are the ones to talk about God's Son and what he can do for people's lives?

My reluctance to talk about my spiritual walk frustrates me. I sometimes indicate that I will pray for a neighbor's health, or their children, or a life situation with which they are struggling at the time. However, I don't question or follow up with how my Lord has answered my needs for the day. Many times the desire to do so surfaces, but I fear getting too personal or leaving the impression that I might be fanatical about my faith. How odd! Most of them think I am fanatical about walking, and that certainly doesn't bother me. So, I ask myself why it should bother me if they think the same about my Christian walking.

I remind myself that my Lord said, "If anyone is ashamed of me and my words, the Son of Man will be ashamed of him when he comes in his glory and in the glory of the Father and of the holy angels" (Luke 9:26). I find encouragement in the words of Paul to Timothy, "God did not give us a spirit of timidity, but a spirit of power, and love, and of self-discipline, so do not be ashamed to testify about our Lord" (2 Tim. 1:7, 8). I must increase this *spirit of power, of love, and of self-discipline* in my daily walk. I must learn to speak without shame whether it be about physical walking or spiritual walking.

PRAYER FOR TODAY

Lord, help me to become as confident in spiritual discussions as I am in discussing earthly matters. Increase my spirit of power, love, and self-discipline. Take away my anxiety in times when I should be confident. I want to be your witness, Lord.

God did not give us a spirit of timidity.
—2 Timothy 1:7

ADDITIONAL SCRIPTURE READING

Mark 8:28; Luke 9:26; 2 Timothy 1:7, 8

WALKING PRECAUTIONS

Always carry some identification in a zippered pocket listing your name, address, phone, emergency contacts, important health conditions, blood type, organ donation preferences, and religious restrictions.

⇒ 30 ⇐

LETTERS IN MY MAILBOX

AFTER MY WALK this morning, I stop at the mailbox to pick up the mail. As I walk toward the house, I shuffle through the envelopes—an advertisement for seed corn, a bill from the electric company, the latest flier from Rural King. Then my excitement mounts—a decorated beige envelope from New Mexico! I know this is just what I need, a letter of love and encouragement from a friend. Her letters are warm, caring, and loving, just like she is. Isn't it interesting how our letters reflect who we really are? The cards we buy, the stationery we use, our handwriting, and the words we choose to place on the page—each choice is a message to our reader. Even Paul, when he wrote his second letter to the Corinthians, referred to the power of letters to illustrate Christianity to the people of his day: "You yourselves are our letter; written on our hearts, known and read by everybody" (2 Cor. 3:2).

Wow! If I am a *letter from Christ* to the world I walk in, what is the world reading? Is my envelope attractive? Do they want to read the contents? Do they find a warm, caring, friendly note or has the envelope deceived them? I wonder.

First impressions are so important. What kind of first impression am I making during my daily Christian walk? Only a good first impression, an inviting salutation, will cause people to continue reading me as a letter from Christ. If as I walk and my clothing becomes more important than my attitude, no one will continue *reading* my life.

And then there is my tongue. Oh my! Without a tight rein on my tongue, many of the people I meet may decide to stop *reading* this letter from Christ. James writes directly to me when he writes, "If anyone considers himself religious and yet does not keep a tight rein on his tongue, he deceives himself and his religion is worthless" (James 1:26).

So how do I choose my words? Paul offers the perfect advice: "Let your conversation be always full of grace, seasoned with salt, so that you may know how to answer everyone" (Col. 4:6), and "Do not let any unwholesome talk come out of your mouths, but only what is helpful for building others up according to their needs, that it may benefit those who listen" (Eph. 4:29).

If a person gets to the body of my letter, does the first impression last? What do the people who read me on my daily walk see? I hope they are *reading* a praying woman, a woman who studies his word, a woman who lives out her faith.

As with all personal or friendly letters, the closing must be with love. All good letter writers know they must read and reread, mark out, revise, and correct their correspondence. I must always be eager to erase, revise, or renew my living letter to the world I walk in each day.

PRAYER FOR TODAY

O Lord, help me to be what you would have me to be. Help me to walk in such a way that when the world reads my life they find your compassion, your forgiveness, and your love. Help me to be the encouraging "letter" in someone's life today.

You yourselves are our letter written in our hearts, known and read by everybody. You show that you are a letter from Christ.
—2 Corinthians 3:2, 3

ADDITIONAL SCRIPTURE READING

Ephesians 4:29; Colossians 3:7; 4:6; James 1:26

> "A good example is the best sermon."
>
> —BENJAMIN FRANKLIN (1706–1790),
> American printer, writer, philosopher, scientist, and inventor

⇒ 31 ⇐

NO GRAPES ON THE VINE?

I WALK WITH plodding steps and heavy heart today. A thirteen-year-old was killed last night while driving a car without permission. Sickness is rampant in our congregation. The bodies of those who have been faithful for so long are wearing out, and many of our young people are leaving the church. Much like Habakkuk, I cry out to the Lord.

Just last night I had read Habakkuk's complaining to God. He wanted answers to some of the same questions I am asking today. "Why are you silent while the wicked swallow up those more righteous than themselves?" (Hab. 1:13). Those complaints sound so familiar that I must remember that Habakkuk of the Old Testament, not a contemporary preacher, voiced them. Why *do* bad things happen to good people? Why *do* the unrighteous often prosper, seemingly untouched by trouble, while my Christian friends suffer daily? How can I rejoice when there is so much unfairness and evil in the world? My mind is full of "whys." It's just not fair Lord!

Like Habakkuk, I question if God is listening. If God *is* listening, things should change shouldn't they? Rain should fall for our dry crops. Our congregation should grow spiritually as well as numerically. My friends should be healed. My students should live in loving families with both parents. Teens should not die needless deaths. Safe city streets should be the norm. My prayer list goes on and on. If God really listens to my cries of help why don't I see signs of change? This morning I cry out, "there is strife, and conflict abounds . . . the wicked hem in the righteous, so that justice is perverted" (Hab. 1:3, 4).

Like the prophet of old, I need to climb into a tower, station myself at the ramparts, and look to see what God will say (see Hab. 2:1). I need to accept God's response and acknowledge that he is omniscient and omnipotent, all-knowing and all-powerful. *Accept* is the key word, and it goes hand in hand with faith. Habakkuk says, "the righteous live by his faith" (Hab. 2:4). Habakkuk certainly had that faith. He writes about rejoicing in God when there appears to be no good reason to do so. I don't know about you, but I struggle to be a servant who rejoices when my world is collapsing around me.

I think of my daughter and son-in-law and their painfully long process of fertility testing and adoption proceedings. After several years of this frustration, they were told all they could do was wait. Rather than just wait, they prayed and prepared for God to answer their prayer. They decorated a nursery and stocked it with supplies. When they were finished, they left the nursery door open. Every day they walked by the "waiting room." Each time I visited, which was often, I struggled with the temptation to close that door. To me it was only a reminder of their years of heartache and disappointment. Days, months—a year went by—but the door to the empty nursery stayed open. They were ready and expecting an answer. One Friday morning they had no child, but by Monday they were parents of a five-month-old son. Sometimes faith is just leaving a door open, literally or symbolically.

I trudge home with a lighter heart. I remind myself that faith is getting ready as best I can, then leaving the door open to God's response—even when other people suggest it might be better closed. I must stand at my *watch* prepared and ready for God's answer to my prayers. Increasing my faith through preparation, spiritual as well as physical, does at times result in failed crops. However, I am surrounded by reminders that God is still in control of his creation and that he will "enable me to go on the heights" even though there are "no grapes on the vines" and "the olive crop fails."

PRAYER FOR TODAY

Lord, give me the wisdom to recognize that in my failures of faith you are present and still listening. Help me to prepare myself to be a person that you can trust with your answer to my prayers. Help my faith to grow that I might be more joyful in God my Savior.

Though the fig tree does not bud and there are no grapes on the vine . . . I will be joyful in God my Savior.
—Habakkuk 3:17, 18

ADDITIONAL SCRIPTURE READING

Habakkuk 1—3

WALKING PRECAUTION

Drink a large glass of water before walking. A cup of water every mile or so will slow dehydration. On longer walks switch to a sports drink that contains salt to maintain your salt balance.

⇒ 32 ⇐

ONE NATION UNDER GOD

I AM DELIGHTED by the calm beauty of the day. The sky is the blue of the old-fashioned crock I use for sliced strawberries, with floating white clouds as whipped cream topping. The sun came up bright orange—no haze, a light breeze—all is well this morning.

Just over the top of the school building is the red, white, and blue of our flag drifting in the breeze. As I start across the schoolyard, small children burst from the building in a mad scramble to be first on the playground. I enjoy the multicolored blurs of energy and the squealing happy laughter bubbling from the mob of vitality before me. How exciting life is for them. They are free to laugh and play, study and grow, or as one little boy is doing, sit under the slide and watch. I watch too, and then wander on toward home.

As I load the dishwasher, the memory of the flag flying and the children laughing intermingles with my thoughts of the young soldier who came forward to be baptized Sunday. He was in uniform, yet he looked so young—just a child in my eyes. Only a few years ago he was a youngster on that playground; now he is headed for the war zone of Iraq.

Mixed emotions fill my heart. Today those children on the playground can play free on American soil. Hunger and pain of war are not a part of their lives. They have the inalienable rights of the Constitution. As a citizen I seldom think on these rights, but I know they exist. How fortunate we all are—the young man, the children, and me—to be American citizens. What an advantage it is to live in a country where we can play and study freely, where being a part of the armed forces is a voluntary action, and most importantly, where we can openly worship God.

This freedom will keep schoolchildren playing and give a young soldier needed support for the future. God's Word commands me to pray for our leaders and those in charge. I stop my daily tasks, go to my Bible, and pray silently for our leaders, for those young people serving away from home, and for future freedom for the youngsters on the playground.

PRAYER FOR TODAY

Lord, give our leaders guidance and understanding that they may do your will as they lead our country. Be with all our armed forces and their families as they serve for us. Give them your peace so that even in the midst of war, they can find a security in your promise that you are always with us, even unto the ends of the world.

I urge then, first of all, that requests, prayers, intercession and thanksgiving be made for everyone—for kings and all those in authority that we may live peaceful and quiet lives in all godliness and holiness.
—1 Timothy 2:1, 2

ADDITIONAL SCRIPTURE READING
Hebrews 13:17

"The role of the teacher remains the highest calling of a free people. To the teacher, America entrusts her most precious resource, her children; and asks that they be prepared . . . to face the rigors of individual participation in a democratic society."

—SHIRLEY MOUNT HUFSTEADER (b. 1925),
U.S. Secretary of Education, 1979–1981

⇒ 33 ⇐

DRY CREEK BED

THE EARTH IS parched. Along the roads, the once green ditches are now clumps of rusty grass, remnants of the hot sun of July and August. As I walk into the woods, the leaves crunch beneath my feet much like dry cereal under my rolling pin. Everything is thirsty, and dawn again brings the bright orange sun of another day of blue sky, white puffy clouds, and a soft breeze.

It is beautiful weather, except we need the rain so much. It is harvest time, and the sound of the tractors in the fields and the sights of the already harvested fields remind me that summer is almost gone. The rain we needed never came. But there is still a harvest! For some, much less than what was expected, but, as always in this area of God's creation, there is a harvest.

When I reach the bridge, the creek bed is dry. I have not walked for a few days, so this is the first time I have seen the peeling gray dirt where a few weeks ago there had been flowing water. The water is gone, and in its place are old tires, broken bottles, an old car muffler, and several rusty beer cans—the refuse of the travelers who passed across the bridge during the past few months. What a mess!

What I see is much like what is in my mind this morning. For days now my mind has been littered with old miseries, broken dreams, and "rusty" worn-out ideas. All of these should be discarded and left alone. Just as the earth in my neighborhood needs the wind and rain to blow away the cobwebs and wet the earth, I need the winds of prayer and the rain of Bible study to saturate my mind and wash away the litter that I have allowed to collect.

Jesus told us to "love the Lord your God with all your heart, with all your soul, and with all your mind" (Mark 12:30). I have confidence that my soul is okay today. I am not too worried about my heart as it is still filled with love and caring for my fellow man. But in my mind thoughts are running rampant. I need to turn things around. God would have me think about: "Whatever is true, whatever is noble, whatever is right, whatever is pure, whatever is lovely, whatever is admirable—if anything is excellent or praiseworthy— think about such things" (Phil. 4:8).

PRAYER FOR TODAY

Help me, Lord, to remove this trash and litter from my mind. Let me feel your Holy Spirit fall on me much like the soft, gentle rain of nature. Help me to fill my mind with your Word and know that it will flood my soul with beauty and goodness. Give me a clean heart and mind.

Create in me a pure heart, O God.
—Psalm 51:10

ADDITIONAL SCRIPTURE READING

Psalm 19:14; 24:4; 73:1; Proverbs 14:30; Matthew 5:8

WARNING FOR WALKERS

Heat sickness is a true medical emergency. Stop and cool down at the first signs of heat sickness.

Signs of dehydration: Dry mouth, fatigue, dizziness, stomachache, back pain, headache, irritability, and decreased urination.

Signs of loss of salt: Nausea, headache, cramps, confusion, slurred speech, bloating, and swollen hands.

⇒ 34 ⇐

I'LL BE RIGHT BACK

S I START down the drive for my morning walk, I notice my husband across the yard and call out, "I'll be right back."

It's our way of saying "good-bye," "see you later," "don't forget me while I'm gone," and all the other encouraging words that couples and families exchange with one another. Many times, if we are to be gone for any period of time, we add, "love you" to our parting remarks. I smile as I walk down the road. My parting words to my husband reminded me of our youngest granddaughter the day before.

Anneke is two years old and has been a part of our family for about five months. When our daughter's family brought her home from Romania, she had been shifted from one spot to another several times, so to assure her that she will never be left again, our daughter always says "I'll be right back," whenever she leaves, even if she is only going from one room to the next. Anneke had never heard a word of English before her adoption, and we understood nothing she said in her baby Romanian, yet, yesterday as she was leaving our table to play in the McDonald's playground, she turned to me, patted my knee in assurance and in well-spoken English declared, "I'll be right back!"

We all smiled! Not only could Anneke say the words quite clearly and in the proper order, she obviously understood their meaning. In a short period of time, she has learned to trust us when we say, "I'll be right back." Even though she may not verbally be able to tell us at her young age, she has grasped the concept that in our family "I'll be right back" means "I love you," "trust me," or "even if I need to go away, I'll be back." This morning I still feel a lump of joy in my throat as I recall her little hand patting me and assuring me of her return.

Sometimes I need to be reminded that Jesus gave me the same assurance in much the same way. As Anneke has so quickly realized, "I'll be right back" is security. When a person she loves tells her this, she trusts them. We, too, need to trust that Jesus is coming right back. He said, "I am going there to prepare a place for you. And if I go and prepare a place for you, I will come back and take you to be with me that you also may be where I am" (John 14:3). What security! What a promise!

Sometimes I get scared and feel lost. At those times it is easy for me to forget that he said he would come back. Just like our little one at times calls for her mother, I call out to him for assurance. I go to his Word. I bow in prayer. I find fellowship with other Christians, and in these things I receive the calm assurance that I'll be all right until he comes back or I go where he is. And just as Anneke's mother soothes her from another room, Jesus calms my fears and assures me that he is with me always (Matt. 28:20) and he will be right back.

PRAYER FOR TODAY

Father, help me be like my granddaughter and learn to trust in your promise to come back. Help me to share your promise with those around me who need to know your truths. I want to live a life that demonstrates my belief in your Word. Make me childlike in my faith.

I will come back and take you to be with me
that you also may be where I am.
—John 14:3

ADDITIONAL SCRIPTURE READING
Matthew 28:30

"God never made a promise that was too good to be true."
—DWIGHT L. MOODY (1837–1899), American evangelist

≥ 35 ≤

WALKING A NEW ROUTE

TODAY, I AM walking one of my new routes. I knew it would happen eventually. My husband and I had talked about buying a smaller place in town for our permanent home and a place in Florida for the winter. Now it is a reality, and I am surprised by my reaction. Change has never been easy for me, and this in-town route is definitely a change. If my neighbor, who is also a morning walker, had offered to walk with me this morning, I would have accepted. However, I have walked for a long time by myself, so I should be able to handle this on my own.

Walking along the edge of the highway bordering our new home, I face the cars speeding toward me. No one waves. No one acknowledges me. I finally turn up a side street that leads me past house after house. I see no woods, no cornfields, no deer in the waterway. When I decide I have covered my daily distance requirement, I cut through the local schoolyard and wander down the alley toward my home.

My walking route is no doubt a minor technicality to my family and friends, but adapting to city streets and traffic is a personal struggle. It really isn't the road that is significant; it's just that it isn't familiar territory; it isn't home. My struggle with different surroundings is only one obstacle. Adjusting to this move is difficult in many ways. The difficulty is not only in the physical changes, but also in the dawning realization that I am beginning the final stages of my earthly life. My *someday* is now my today. How exciting, yet how frightening!

I think about what a new environment, a new life entails. People just beginning the Christian life—no matter what their age—must feel a similar mixture of excitement and fear. I, who have been raised in the church, don't realize (or I just forget) how exciting, yet frightening new life with Christ can be. Jesus said, "Behold, I make all things new," but I never really experienced a dramatic change from old to new. Yet the route of daily Christian living is not familiar to any new believers. Much like my experience in walking my new route, they are walking in entirely new territory. Perhaps their old routes led through paths of alcohol, wastelands of drugs, or valleys of depression, all experienced without the saving grace of Jesus. Wherever they have traveled previously, a change to new surroundings, new choices, and a new course in life is difficult.

Not only do new believers walk a different path in new surroundings, but also the vocabulary of their new environment may be as strange as the new road. Common terms in the Christian world may be foreign to a newcomer. "Saving grace," for example, is not a term commonly used or understood in the secular world, and it may be a stumbling block for new Christian travelers.

Even worship services can become a struggle for the newcomer. When Christians gather for worship services, we usually expect everyone to know what to do, what to say, when to stand, and when to sit. Even though these practices are small pebbles on the new route, they can seem like boulders to a stranger on the worship road. Just as no one waved or acknowledged me on my new walking route, so we veteran churchgoers may also ignore the beginning worshiper.

The physical changes in my life, much like the changes in the life of the new Christian, are exciting as well as frightening. Whenever a person leaves the familiar to journey into the exciting unknown, some apprehension is present. Walking with a companion can be such a comfort. Words of encouragement and invitations for fellowship make a difference. The opportunity to share common experiences through the week rather than just Sunday is important for all believers, especially for those who are making a change in life. Even though I am an experienced walker, changing to an unfamiliar route was difficult. Rather than learning through trial and error, beginning believers benefit greatly when a loving, patient friend who is familiar with the route can guide them on the path. Anyone who is making changes in life needs encouragement and understanding from fellow walkers.

PRAYER FOR TODAY

Help me, Lord, to accept the changes in my life and to be more encouraging and understanding of those around me who are also making changes in their lives. Help me to say or do something that will make a new Christian aware of the joy and satisfaction they will experience because of the changes they are making with you and your people.

Just as Christ was raised from the dead through the
glory of the Father, we too may live a new life.
—Romans 6:4

ADDITIONAL SCRIPTURE READING
Ephesians 4:24

"A man travels the world over in search of
what he needs and returns home to find it."

—GEORGE MOORE, Irish author, dramatist, and poet

⇒ 36 ⇐

WALKING IN SUNSHINE

I AM WALKING in sunlight! It surrounds me and seeps into my body like warm butter on a hot biscuit. The warmth is a comfort rather like snuggling under an electric blanket on a cold night. My stiff muscles of yesterday begin to flow smoothly. Each step I take in the Florida morning sunlight is a joy to both body and soul. I so appreciate this light and warmth after the dark and cold of our northern winter.

Treading the sidewalks of our mobile home park, I mentally embrace the familiar surroundings that greet me on my return each winter. The yellow and red hibiscus flowers flow into the green grass surrounding the pool area. I pause to watch two young visitors (no doubt someone's grandchildren) as they splash in the sun-sparkled water. Across the way, a fellow *snowbird* waves hello, and the neighbors of last year greet me with welcoming smiles and open arms.

Walking in this sunlight is similar to walking in God's love: it surrounds and envelops. The sunshine grows hotter and more intense as the day goes on. We raise our blinds, and throw open doors and windows to let the wonderful light and warmth invade our home. We soak up the warmth much like a sponge soaks up the water around it.

Likewise, walking in the sunshine of God's love means leaving the "cold" of the world and experiencing warmth that absorbs all the cares of life. I can throw open the door of my heart, uncover all my sins, and let God's love fill my soul. Held in his hands and encompassed by his love, I soak up God's love the same way I soak up the Florida sunshine—joyfully.

The comfort of knowing I have a loving heavenly Father who daily surrounds me with his love permeates my soul—just as the sunshine saturates my body. Joy and peace become a part of me that grows hotter and more intense as I become older. The longer I walk with the Lord, the more I realize how the unwavering warmth of his love for me has changed my life from a winter existence to a constant walking in the sunshine of his love.

PRAYER FOR TODAY

I just praise you and thank you for the warmth of the sun on my back today, but more than that Lord, thank you for the sunshine of your love in my life. Thank you, Lord, for causing my life to be one of sunshine and joy. Be with me and all those who love you and bask in your Sonshine.

God is love, and whoever lives in love lives in God, and God in him.
—1 John 4:16

ADDITIONAL SCRIPTURE READING
Psalm 103:11–18; Romans 5:8; Ephesians 2:4, 5

WALKING IN HOT WEATHER

- Never walk in sun without a hat.
- Soak a neck cooler in cold water and wear around neck.
- Powder your feet and areas of chafing before walking in hot weather.
- Owning a good pair of sunglasses is important.

GREEN LIGHTS

TODAY I LEFT my Florida winter home to walk the sidewalks of the surrounding city. As I walk along the uneven concrete, exhaust fumes from the city bus mingle with the frying fish odor from the local Long John Silver's. Honking horns and squealing brakes merge with the sirens of ever-present emergency vehicles in a dissonant chorus of metropolitan sounds. So many people going so many different ways, and all of them are strangers to me and also to one another. What a change from my rural walks of the past. I stop for the red light at the corner. Surrounded by other pedestrians, I wait for the green; it turns, and we all move as one to the opposite curb. An emergency vehicle screams by, and I mentally offer a short prayer for the personnel in the vehicle and their patient. I remember how significant traffic lights and sirens have been in my personal life.

Recently, my husband suffered some severe head pains. It was later diagnosed as a leaking blood vessel at the base of the brain that immediately sealed. When this trauma occurred, he was quite a distance from our house but managed to drive home where I immediately called 911. The sound of sirens and the calm, trained personnel who responded are always a reassuring memory for me. I praised God that day for bringing us to an urban location because immediate response in our rural home area is impossible.

Several days after this incident, doctors questioned my husband about it—how he felt, how he possibly could have driven, and many other seemingly insignificant questions. He remembered thinking how wonderful it was that every stoplight turned green as he approached it. Traveling any distance in the local traffic without a red stoplight is unusual. Most people say it is unheard of, yet that is what happened. Some might say "how lucky," but my husband and I personally praise God for that blessing.

I am reminded of green lights again today as I walk the sidewalks of the city. I wonder how many green lights God provides in my life that I am not even aware of. I know that Satan throws up roadblocks and stoplights daily. Paul told the people at Ephesus that "our struggle is not against flesh and blood, but against the rulers, against the authorities, against the powers of this dark world and against the spiritual forces of evil in the heavenly realms" (Eph. 6:12). Although many people would consider all those green lights to be a coincidence, I know God cares for his people. It is not luck that provides green lights in our lives. As Christian people, we must publicly announce God's blessings even in the simplest happenings of our days. Green lights must be acknowledged and pointed out to the people around us. It is in these simple, day-to-day events that we can truly witness to the multitude of strangers who walk beside us down the sidewalk of life.

PRAYER FOR TODAY

Thank you, Lord, for the way you take care of my family and me. Thank you for the times that you have provided green lights for us both literally and figuratively. I praise you, Lord, for all your daily care and blessings that I sometimes forget to acknowledge. I know you are always watching over your children as they battle in this world. Thank you for that.

I will fear no evil for you are with me.
—Psalm 23:4

ADDITIONAL SCRIPTURE READING
Matthew 10:28–33; 1 Peter 5:7

"Miracles are a retelling in small letters of the very
same story which is written across the whole world
in letters too large for some of us to see."

—C. S. LEWIS (1898–1963), author, *Miracles*

⇒ 38 ⇐

BEACH WALKING

I AM BEACH WALKING today. What a treat! The cool, crunchy feeling of sand and broken shells is such a unique experience for someone from the cornfields of Illinois that I indulge myself by stopping to wiggle my bare toes in the sand. The hot sun beating down on my shoulder blades soaks into my aching muscles, and I hesitate just long enough to stretch toward its welcome warmth. I never cease to be amazed by the warmth and beauty of the beach. I am enticed by the promise of the breeze at sunrise and the relaxation of a day on the beach.

The encroaching tide laps at my wiggling toes, and I move down the beach at a more vigorous pace. Many other walkers join me on my morning trek. Although we are strangers, we often acknowledge a fellow sojourner with a hesitant nod or a brief smile. Walking with others in such an environment is a new experience for me, but I rather enjoy it. Walking alone previously has been essential for my devotional time to be meaningful, but today something about the hodgepodge of humanity walking beside the incessant rolling of the waves reminds me that there really *are* constants in this world. The building of sandcastles by frolicking children, lovers entwined in a morning embrace, the sun rising on the horizon, the waves breaking on the shore are all ageless, yet each one is new. I rest on the sand and reflect on all that surrounds me. The unceasing waves remind me of God's unending love. I don't understand how any of it really happens—the waves or God's love—but I can see the results of both on the beach this morning, and my experience tells me that both will continue.

Taking my Bible from my beach bag, I read John 3:16 that God so loved that world that he sent his Son to die for me and for all generations. I also read, "Jesus Christ is the same yesterday, and today, and forever" (Heb. 13:8). What a promise! How much easier it is for me to understand and believe these promises as I sit on the beach and experience the constant beating of the waves against the shoreline. All of God's creation is so complex, yet so simple. Just as I know the next wave is going to roll in, I know God loves me. I find comfort in that.

I watch the movements of the sea gulls as they repeatedly soar and dive over the waves. I gaze at the horizon that stretches beyond my imagination. The depth and breadth of the ocean is a trite phrase, but how else can one describe this awesome creation? Even though the psalmists so often attempted to express the depth and breadth of God's love, they, like me, find it difficult to characterize.

But I have proof of God's love for me in his son Jesus Christ. As I linger here this morning, I think again and again of Paul's words in Hebrews as he writes, "Jesus Christ is the same yesterday, and today, and forever." Just like the scenes before me are ageless, so, too, is the promise of the Scriptures. God and his Son and their love for me will never change. I leave the beach encouraged and uplifted by the illustrations of this unending love that I behold in God's creation.

PRAYER FOR TODAY

Lord, keep me aware of how much you really love me. Remind me that the world around me may change, but Christ and his death on the cross will never change. I want to be aware of your promises as I see them in your creation. Thank you for the beauty of the beach and the privilege to be a part of your creation.

Jesus Christ is the same yesterday, and today, and forever.
—Hebrews 13:8

ADDITIONAL SCRIPTURE READING

2 Chronicles 5:13; John 3:16

"Renew thyself completely each day;
do it again, and again, and forever again."

—Chinese inscription cited by Henry Thoreau in *Walden*

≥ 39 ≤

GOING HOME

I WALK ALONG THE sidewalk in our mobile home park inhaling the odor of the orange blossoms. The lingering sweet aroma is an exotic, exhilarating fragrance—especially to a Midwest native. The plants, birds, blue skies, wonderful sunshine, beaches—all are such a contrast to the environment I call home.

All of nature here is so different than Illinois. I take great delight in the citrus fruit trees and the flowering shrubs that are a part of the landscape. I smile as I notice the white skinny-legged bird digging with its pointed beak in my Florida sod. The bright pinks and cheerful yellows of the hibiscus blooming on my street are foreign to the locale of my childhood. This truly is a beautiful place, and I love it during the winter months. I have cherished friends here. It's a wonderful way of life, but despite my feelings of enjoyment and satisfaction, I am still not at home. Home is in Illinois where I belong.

I could describe life on earth in similar ways. I love my life on earth. I want it to last as long as possible. I have visited and enjoyed much of God's creation. My church family is a great delight to me. God has blessed me with the love of a good man, and our children have blessed us. My life on earth is good, but just as Florida is not my home, neither is this world.

Throughout Scripture we are told that we are not to be of this "world." Paul reminded the Philippians, "Our citizenship is in heaven" (Phil. 3:20). We are here on earth to prepare for eternity. So Paul continued his comments about our true citizenship by encouraging us to "eagerly await the Savior" who will "transform our lowly bodies so that they will be like his glorious body" (Phil. 3:20, 21).

As I finish my walk, I sit alone by the pool and consider Paul's admonition to "stand firm in the Lord." I think of the heavenly home I have been promised—eternal life in a home that is beyond my comprehension. My anticipation for our trip home to Illinois pales in comparison to the journey I will one day make to my home in eternity.

PRAYER FOR TODAY

Lord, I do appreciate and thank you for the home I have here on earth. I thank you for the good life I have. But most of all, I want to thank you for the promise you have given me that someday I can walk home to you and your Son, Jesus Christ.

Our citizenship is in heaven.
—Philippians 3:20

ADDITIONAL SCRIPTURE READING
John 14:2; John 14:23; Ephesians 2:10

"Two roads diverged in a wood and I took the one less traveled by, And that has made all the difference."

—ROBERT FROST (1874–1963), *The Road Not Taken*